D0105923

TABLE OF CONTENTS

Unless otherwise indicated, all Scripture quotations are taken from the King James Version of the Bible.

7 Decisions That Will Decide Your Success In Life · ISBN 1-56394-434-0/B-295

Copyright © 2010 by **MIKE MURDOCK**

Publisher/Editor: Deborah Murdock Johnson

Published by The Wisdom Center · 4051 Denton Hwy. · Ft. Worth, Texas 76117

1-817-759-BOOK · 1-817-759-2665 · 1-817-759-0300

You Will Love Our Website..! WisdomOnline.com

Accuracy Department: To our Friends and Partners...We welcome any comments on errors or misprints you find in our book...Email our department: AccuracyDept@thewisdomcenter.tv. Your aid in helping us excel is highly valued.

Your Decisions
Decide Your Success
In Life.

-MIKE MURDOCK

Why I Wrote This Book

The Word of God Is The Wisdom of God.

Proverbs 4:7 states, "Wisdom is the principal thing; therefore get Wisdom."

Wisdom Is The Ability To Recognize Difference. Difference between right and wrong...in people...in an environment...in a countenance.

When Joseph looked at the countenance of the butler and the baker, he saw Difference. "And Joseph came in unto them in the morning, and looked upon them, and, behold, they were sad," (Genesis 40:6).

When Jesus hung between two thieves, *one* recognized His Difference. "And one of the malefactors which were hanged railed on Him, saying, If Thou be Christ, save Thyself and us. But the other answering rebuked him, saying, Dost not thou fear God, seeing thou art in the same condemnation? And we indeed justly; for we receive the due reward of our deeds: but this Man hath done nothing amiss," (Luke 23:39-41).

There is a popular teaching that God is in control of everything. He decides everything.

But is God really in control of everything?

I walked up to a preacher who had been teaching this in a conference. He said, "God is in control!"

I asked, "Of what?"

He replied, "God is in control of everything."

"Really? Everything that happens was planned by God?"

"Yes. Everything."

"So, if a woman is raped we cannot prosecute the *rapist* because God was in control? If a man was murdered you cannot prosecute the *murderer* because God was in control?"

"I had not thought about that."

If everything that happens is decided by God, what is the purpose of Wisdom...*the ability to recognize Difference.*

What is the reward of *knowledge?* What is the benefit of *obedience?* If God has already planned everything, why pursue teaching?

Nothing would bring more comfort than to think *everything* that happens was planned by God. However, this philosophy removes the burden of *Decision-Making* from you and me, making God responsible. The fact remains *Your Decisions* are deciding your Future and the *quality* of your life.

God has given you that responsibility. "Choose you this day whom ye will serve," (Joshua 24:15).

Your Decisions Decide Your Success In Life.

That is why I wrote this book.

Mike Murdock

1

YOUR DECISION TO BUILD YOUR FAITH

Your Faith Decides Your Experiences.

Faith is something that can be *built.* You can cause *Small* faith to become *Great* faith.

God is not responsible for your faith. You are responsible for your faith. Why is faith important?

Faith is the only thing that produces Miracles.

God has never responded…to *pain.*

God has never responded…to *tears.*

God has never responded…to a *human problem.*

God responds to *faith.*

Faith Is The Only Voice God Respects.

What is God like? The character of God is hidden in Numbers 23. It explains the character of God…His *behavior*…His *conduct*…His *personality.* "God is not a man, that He should lie; neither the son of man, that He should repent: hath He said, and shall He not do it? or hath He spoken, and shall He not make it good?" (Numbers 23:19).

God has one obsession…*to be believed.* God craves to be trusted. He becomes angry when He is doubted. *God's Only Pain Is To Be Doubted; God's Only Pleasure Is To Be Believed.*

Everything good God has planned for you will not

happen *until* you trust Him. "But let him ask in faith, nothing wavering. For he that wavereth is like a wave of the sea driven with the wind and tossed. For let not that man think that he shall receive any thing of the Lord," (James 1:6-7).

What Makes Doubt So Deadly..?

Doubt Produces Tragedies As Quickly As Faith Produces Miracles.

Twelve spies went to Canaan. They spied out the land for 40 days. Ten men came back full of doubt and unbelief. For every *day* of doubt, God gave them a *year* of heartache. "And your children shall wander in the wilderness forty years, and bear your whoredoms, until your carcases be wasted in the wilderness. After the number of the days in which ye searched the land, even forty days, each day for a year, shall ye bear your iniquities, even forty years, and ye shall know My breach of promise," (Numbers 14:33-34).

Doubt Produces Pain Like Faith Produces Miracles. If you do not get into faith, you will get into doubt. I did not get into faith because I wanted to own a Rolls Royce. I got into faith because I did not want to experience the tragedies doubt produces.

Doubt Authorizes Satanic Attack Against Your Life. Doubt leaves you stripped of protection.

3 Faith Reminders

Faith comes when you hear God talk.
Faith is *confidence* in God.
Faith is *voice-activated.* Faith is not a silent voice inside you. Faith must be released with your mouth.

You cannot even be saved until you speak. "That if thou shalt confess with thy mouth the Lord Jesus, and shalt believe in thine heart that God hath raised Him from the dead, thou shalt be saved. For with the heart man believeth unto righteousness; and with the mouth confession is made unto salvation," (Romans 10:9-10).

How Do You Build Your Faith..?

Faith comes by hearing...*the words of God.*

God has hidden *trust capability* in His words.

When I hear something God says, faith rises in me. Every morning I listen to The Bible on my iPod.

What Enters You Determines What Exits You.

How do you get darkness to *leave* a room? You turn on the light and the *entry* of the light forces the *exit* of the darkness.

This is The Law of Displacement.

Daniel put it this way. "How does a man break off iniquity? By acts of righteousness." (See Daniel 4:27.)

How do I cause doubt to leave? *By bringing faith in.* When God begins to talk, doubt and fear *die.*

Every decision you make will be from *fear* or *faith.* You must develop your *own* faith...others will contribute to your *doubts.*

Build your faith.

Nurture your faith.

Saturate your Mind with The Word of God. All doubt will be dispelled. Every word that enters your ear should be Faith-Talk.

The greatest chapter in The Bible is Psalm 119. It talks about what The Word of God will do in your life. "Thy word is a lamp unto my feet, and a light unto my path," (Psalm 119:105).

Top 10 Facts About Faith

▶ *Your Faith Decides Your Experiences.*

▶ *Faith Is The Only Voice God Respects.*

▶ *God's Only Pain Is To Be Doubted; God's Only Pleasure Is To Be Believed.*

▶ *Doubt Produces Tragedies As Quickly As Faith Produces Miracles.*

▶ *Doubt Produces Pain Like Faith Produces Miracles.*

▶ *Doubt Authorizes Satanic Attack In Your Life.*

▶ *What Enters You Determines What Exits You.*

▶ *Every Decision You Make Will Be From Fear or Faith.*

▶ *Faith Is Voice-Activated.*

▶ *Faith Comes When You Hear God Talk.*

RECOMMENDED INVESTMENTS:
Seeds of Wisdom on Faith-Talk, Vol. 12 (Book/B-24/32 pg/$3)
The God Book (Book/B-26/160 pg/$10)
The Seeds of Wisdom Topical Bible (Book/B-31/368 pg/$10)
31 Greatest Chapters In The Bible (Book/B-54/138 pg/$10)
The Book That Changed My Life, Vol. 15 (Book/B-117A/32 pg/$7)

2

YOUR DECISION TO EXCEL IN YOUR PRESENT ASSIGNMENT

Everything Created Solves A Problem.
My eyes *see.*
My ears *hear.*
My mouth *speaks.*
My Mind *thinks.*
My hands *reach.*
My feet *walk.*
Lawyers solve *legal* problems.
Mothers solve *emotional* problems.
Preachers solve *spiritual* problems.

The fact that you are alive on the earth is proof that God saw a problem nobody else could solve...*but you.* That is your Assignment. *Your Assignment Is Always The Problem God Has Designed You To Solve For Others.*

You do not choose it.
You *recognize* it.
You do not decide who you are.
You *discern* who He made you.
Turtles do not talk. Trees do not fly.
Your Assignment Is Not Your Decision – But Your Discovery. Design reveals purpose.

What you hate is a clue to your Assignment.

Why did Moses become angry when he saw an Israelite physically beaten by an Egyptian? Because Moses was a Deliverer. "And it came to pass in those days, when Moses was grown, that he went out unto his brethren, and looked on their burdens: and he spied an Egyptian smiting an Hebrew, one of his brethren. And he looked this way and that way, and when he saw that there was no man, he slew the Egyptian, and hid him in the sand," (Exodus 2:11-12).

Love is a path and a clue to a hidden gift. What do you love to *think* about...*learn* about? Pay attention to what you love. What you love is a clue to your Assignment.

The Proof of Love Is The Investment of Time.

What grieves you is a clue to your Assignment.

What makes you weep is a clue to something God wants you to change and heal.

Make Your Assignment Your Obsession

Your Assignment must become your obsession.

You Will Only Have Significant Success In Something That Is An Obsession.

You will only succeed in the *center* of your Assignment. It is possible for a sinner to be in the center of his Assignment. It is also possible for a Christian to fail at recognizing his own Assignment.

Your Assignment is *geographical.*

God Made Places Before He Made People.

Even Jesus did not do well in certain places. That is why He left Nazareth and went to Capernaum. "And He did not many mighty works there because of their unbelief," (Matthew 13:58). *Go Where You Are*

Celebrated Instead of Where You Are Tolerated.

Divine Conversations Involve A Place

It happened for Elijah in 1 Kings 17. "Get thee hence, and turn thee eastward, and hide thyself by the brook Cherith, that is before Jordan. And it shall be, that thou shalt drink of the brook; and I have commanded the ravens to feed thee there. Arise, get thee to Zarephath, which belongeth to Zidon, and dwell there: behold, I have commanded a widow woman there to sustain thee," (1 Kings 17:3-4, 9).

Your Success is *connected* to a Place.

Your Assignment is to a *Place.*

You will *flourish* when you are in the center of where God assigns you.

A vendor brought some fish out to my property. Before I put them in the ponds, they just lay on the grass gasping. I thought, "Wow, they are stupid. They cannot walk. They cannot talk. They cannot fly. Fish are stupid. Maybe I should not eat fish."

When I dropped the fish in the water, their *genius* emerged. God spoke to me, "When you are where I have assigned you, no one can compete with you. You have no *rivals* when you are in the center of your Assignment."

Your Assignment is important because it is the only place God has *guaranteed* Financial Provision.

Money does not follow you. Money is *waiting* for you at the place of your Assignment. Money is the Scriptural *incentive* for obedience.

Everywhere there is Obedience...there is Money.

Everywhere there is Rebellion...there is Loss.

Divine Provision Is Only Guaranteed At The Place

of Your Assignment.

God tells Elijah, "Go to the brook. I have commanded a raven to feed you there." Later, the brook dried up. *Why?* His Assignment had *changed.* "Now go to Zarephath."

Money is geographical.

Jesus stood on the shore and shouted to the disciples, "Children, have you any meat?"

"We have toiled all night and caught nothing."

"You are fishing in the wrong place. Cast your net on the other side." (See John 21:4-6.)

Money Is Waiting For You...At Your Place of Assignment.

Top 10 Facts About Your Assignment

▶ *Everything Created Solves A Problem.*
▶ *Your Assignment Is Always The Problem God Has Designed You To Solve For Others.*
▶ *Your Assignment Is Not Your Decision – But Your Discovery.*
▶ *The Proof of Love Is The Investment of Time.*
▶ *You Will Only Have Significant Success In Something That Is An Obsession.*
▶ *God Made Places Before He Made People.*
▶ *Go Where You Are Celebrated Instead of Where You Are Tolerated.*
▶ *Divine Provision Is Only Guaranteed At The Place of Your Assignment.*
▶ *Money Is Waiting For You...At Your Place of Assignment.*
▶ *Your Assignment Will Always Have An Adversary.*
▶ *Your Assignment Is A Place of Divine Reward.*

3

YOUR DECISION TO HONOR THE SCRIPTURAL CHAIN OF AUTHORITY

The Function of Authority Is Order.

The Divine purpose of Authority is not control. How do you determine the legitimacy of Authority? *The Proofs of Legitimate Authority Are Provision, Protection And Promotion.*

Authority is important in the chain of financial prosperity. Money does not flow up. Money flows down. Money follows the Chain of Authority.

The only person who can promote you is the person in Authority over you.

You Can Only Be Promoted By The Person You Serve. If you remove yourself from the umbrella of that Authority, you remove yourself from Provision, Protection and Promotion. *Your Greatness Is Not Hidden To The One God Has Assigned To Promote You.*

The fifth commandment is the first with a *promise* of a reward. If you honor your mother and father, it will go well with you. "Honour thy father and thy mother, as the Lord thy God hath commanded thee; that thy days may be prolonged, and that it may go well with thee, in the land which the Lord thy God giveth thee," (Deuteronomy 5:16).

You do not have to study at 50 universities to succeed. If you just honor your mother and father, the blessing will come down.

Your reaction to Authority determines how God reacts to you. *Your Reaction To Your Parents Determines God's Reaction To You.*

Years ago, The Holy Spirit began to deal with me about calling my mother and father every day as *proof* of my Honor.

Honoring Parents Guarantees Generational Blessing.

Becoming a year older is not going to increase the blessings in your life! Doing something *different* than you did *last* year will bring down the blessing. *When You Want Something You Have Never Had, You Must Do Something You Have Never Done.*

Follow This Instruction Over The Next 12 Months...

Make a decision to honor those in Authority over your life. Call your mother and father every single day of your life.

Thank them...*for bringing you into the world.*

Thank them...*for teaching you to talk, walk and eat.*

If you will begin to show respect and honor for the Chain of Authority, it will go well with you.

Honor Must Become Your Seed Before You Reap It As A Harvest.

Make a commitment to do this for 12 months and see what happens supernaturally. It is astounding how God began to bless my life when I began to understand

The Law of Honor.

2 Parts of The Gospel

The Gospel has two parts: the Person of Jesus and the Principles of Jesus.

The *Person* of Jesus prepares you for *Eternity*.

The *Principles* of Jesus prepare you for *Earth*.

The *Person* of Jesus creates your *Peace*.

The *Laws* of Jesus create your *Prosperity*.

Every Law produces a different *reward*...a different *fruit*. There are 72 dominant Laws in Scripture. These include...

The Law of *Faith*.

The Law of *Focus*.

The Law of *Love*.

The Law of *Protocol*.

The Law of *Reproduction*.

The Law of *Reward...and so on*.

Each Law produces a reward that a God-experience alone does not produce.

The Law of Reward deals with your *understanding* of money.

I am hesitant to pray for money. Why? Prayer is not the Seed for money. Almost every intercessor I know is broke. I rarely pray for money. I pray for opportunity to Sow...and call in the Harvests.

Money is not...a *Miracle*.

Money is not...a *Mystery*.

Money Is Merely A Reward For Solving A Problem.

When you solve a problem, you create favor. Everywhere you find favor...you find money. *When You Solve A Problem, You Schedule A Reward.*

Honor The Chain of Authority

When I embraced the understanding of the Chain of Authority, something supernatural happened in my life. Make a decision to honor the Authority God has placed over you.

Celebration Is The Proof of Honor.

Top 10 Facts About Authority

▶ *The Divine Purpose For Authority Is Order.*
▶ *The Proofs of Legitimate Authority Are Provision, Protection And Promotion.*
▶ *You Can Only Be Promoted By The Person You Serve.*
▶ *Your Greatness Is Not Hidden To The One God Has Assigned To Promote You.*
▶ *Your Reaction To Your Parents Determines God's Reaction To You.*
▶ *Honoring Parents Guarantees Generational Blessing.*
▶ *When You Want Something You Have Never Had, You Must Do Something You Have Never Done.*
▶ *Honor Must Become Your Seed Before You Reap It As A Harvest.*
▶ *When You Solve A Problem, You Schedule A Reward.*
▶ *Celebration Is The Proof of Honor.*

RECOMMENDED INVESTMENTS:
31 Secrets For Career Success (Book/B-44/114 pg/$10)
The Law of Recognition (Book/B-114/247 pg/$15)
7 Laws You Must Honor To Create Uncommon Success
    (CD/WCPL-327/$10)

≈ 4 ≈

Your Decision To Pursue An Uncommon Mentor

——————⊰•○•⊱——————

Mentorship Is Wisdom Without The Pain.

There are two ways to get Wisdom: People or Pain...*Mentors or Mistakes.*

A mother warns her child, "Do not touch the stove!" The child ignores the warning and gets burned. He learns through *pain* what he does not learn through his *mother.*

Mothers are often Master Mentors. Every man trusts a woman. That is how law enforcement agents locate criminals. When they break out of prison, they will find the woman they trusted. No man can stay *away* from a woman he trusts.

Every man is listening to a woman...a rebellious woman or a woman of Honor.

The Future of Every Man Is Determined By The Woman He Trusts.

My success today is because of a remarkable Mentor...*my mother.* She taught me that my *willingness* to listen to correction would *stop* a lot of *tears*...a lot of *pain*...a lot of *heartache.*

She taught me that Elisha stayed in the presence

of Elijah, Timothy was the protégé of Paul, and Esther was the protégé of Mordecai. Ruth was willing to listen to Naomi. Ruth found her Boaz, because she listened to her Mentor.

Mentorship Is The Transference of Knowledge.

Mentorship is...learning through the pain another has experienced.

Mentorship is...Wisdom without the season of waiting.

An Uncommon Future Requires An Uncommon Mentor.

Whose voice matters to you?

Whose voice do you trust?

Who do you reach for when you hit a crisis?

3 Keys To Uncommon Mentorship

1. Master One Topic. What do you want to know a lot about? *You Will Only Have Significant Success With Something That Is An Obsession.*

My father is obsessed with hearing The Voice of The Spirit. He does not understand Financial Prosperity, but he understands The Voice of The Holy Spirit. I sit at His feet to learn how to be sensitive to God's Voice.

We have met daily for hours in my Secret Place. I have often said, "Daddy, just talk to me." I want to know what he knows that I do not know. (I recorded the revelation that Daddy shared with me in The Secret Place and it is available in a 500 page book, *Truth Out In The Open.)*

Everybody Sees Something You Do Not See.

You cannot eat enough carrots to see behind your

head. You need somebody else who sees what you do not see. Somebody knows what you do not know. You must decide what you want to master.

2. Ask Questions Relentlessly. The most powerful thing on earth is a question. I never look for answers. I look for questions. Questions will introduce you to answers.

Questions Host Answers On The Earth; Answers Only Respond To Questions.

There is nothing on earth more powerful than a question. *Questions Are The Seeds For Wisdom.*

God shares only one conversation Jesus had during His first 30 years on the earth. His reaction to His mother and father was, "Must I not be about My Father's business?" Jesus loved questions so much He answered questions with questions. (See Luke 2:46-52.)

Take one hour during the next 7 days and write out a list of questions. Your life will change dramatically. The questions you ask will decide the seasons you enter.

Questions Schedule Events On The Earth.

If I were my enemy, how would I destroy me?

If I had one night left on the earth, who would I want to be praying with me on my deathbed?

Who are the two people that want my advice and not my money?

In whose presence am I energized?

Who trusts me more than everyone else?

Who am I able to trust?

God's greatest pleasure is to be trusted.

3. Mentorship Will Require Pursuit. Pursuing an Uncommon Mentor will cost you time, criticism and agitation; but the payoff is worth it. You are reading this today because you are pursuing Uncommon Mentorship.

Mentorship matters.

You will avoid a lot of pain through Mentorship.

Document what you listen to.

Listen to teaching CDs. Absorb.

I bought a little book for $84. A young man with me said, "I cannot believe you bought a book for $84."

I replied, "Son, I did not. I bought a man's life. What took him 70 years to learn, I will know in two hours."

Time is not a teacher.

Time has never taught anybody.

Top 10 Facts About Mentorship

▶ *Mentorship Is Wisdom Without The Pain.*

▶ *The Future of Every Man Is Determined By The Woman He Trusts.*

▶ *Mentorship Is The Transference of Knowledge.*

▶ *An Uncommon Future Requires An Uncommon Mentor.*

▶ *You Will Only Have Significant Success With Something That Is An Obsession.*

▶ *Everybody Sees Something You Do Not See.*

▶ *Questions Host Answers On The Earth; Answers Only Respond To Questions.*

▶ *Questions Are The Seeds For Wisdom.*

▶ *Questions Schedule Events On The Earth.*

▶ *An Uncommon Life Will Require An Uncommon Mentor.*

5

YOUR DECISION TO LOOK FOR DIVINE REWARDS IN EVERY BATTLE

Everything Good Is Hated By Everything Evil.
You will not escape battles. Jesus had enemies. You will have enemies. "Remember the word that I said unto you, The servant is not greater than his lord. If they have persecuted Me, they will also persecute you; if they have kept My saying, they will keep yours also," (John 15:20).

You Never Outgrow Warfare; You Must Simply Learn To Fight.

An Enemy is anyone who wants to diminish your influence...*to stop your voice.* No one was more capable at communication than Jesus, *yet He was despised.*

Earth is an *adversarial* environment. Even in The Garden, Adam and Eve had an Adversary. You must look for the Divine Rewards in the battle. You will not enter Canaan without having to confront giants. *Warfare Is The Proof An Enemy Has Discerned Your Future.*

Giants are *signposts.* You will not see giants when you are in Egypt. Giants are clues you have just entered your Canaan. When you discern an Adversary, *get excited.* Giants are an announcement the "grapes" are not far off.

Before David saw Goliath, he was attending to sheep and handling manure. The moment he saw Goliath, he saw a *gate* to the throne.

Your Goliath is your Golden Gate...to success.

Between you and your Future is an Adversary.

In my book, *The Law of Recognition,* I deal with 92 facts about your enemy. (No greater book has ever been written...visit my website for more information at WisdomOnline.com.)

Your Enemy Decides Your Rewards

In the last book of The Bible, Revelation, the only people God blesses and promotes are overcomers. Until you have an enemy, God is not authorized to promote you or bless you. *The Size of Your Enemy Reveals The Size of Your Rewards.*

Make a decision to examine every battle for potential rewards. Look at your enemy *carefully.*

I love what Napoleon Bonaparte said, "Never interrupt an enemy while he is making mistakes."

Your enemy *will* make mistakes.

Your Victories Are Hidden In The Mistakes of Your Enemy.

Top 10 Facts You Should Know About Enemies

▶ *Everything Good Is Hated By Everything Evil.*
▶ *You Never Outgrow Warfare; You Must Simply Learn To Fight.*
▶ *Warfare Is The Proof An Enemy Has Discerned*

Your Future.
▶ *The Size of Your Enemy Reveals The Size of Your Rewards.*
▶ *Your Victories Are Hidden In The Mistakes of Your Enemy.*
▶ *An Enemy Is Not A Wall; An Enemy Is A Door To Your Next Season.*
▶ *An Enemy Is A Magnet For Right People.*
▶ *When Enemies Come Against You, Right People Emerge Around You.*
▶ *An Enemy Exposes Disloyalty And Purges Relationships Within Your Circle.*
▶ *When An Adversary Enters Your Environment, Every False And Shallow Friendship Is Exposed.*

Conversations Decide Your Success or Failure.

-MIKE MURDOCK

6

Your Decision To Continuously Listen To The Voice Of The Holy Spirit

God Rules The Universe Through Conversation.

A few years ago, I was involved in a real estate transaction with a cantankerous and agitating seller. He was 93 years old. He did not really care if the property sold or not. I *desperately* wanted the property, so I kept making one concession after another to his many demands.

Finally, the day came for me to sign the real estate contract. That morning I prayed in The Secret Place, "Father, I really do not feel good about this property any more. I have fought and fought, and now he is willing to let me buy it."

The Holy Spirit replied, "I am not in this transaction. There is no Favor. You have made all the changes, yet he is not willing to make any concessions."

God began to teach me to always follow the path of Favor. Favor is a clue God is involved. *The Path of Favor Is The Will of God.*

The Holy Spirit said, "There is no Favor. You have made all the concessions. He has made none."

I said, "I do not know how to stop the transaction. I have already made my promise. We are going to sign on it today. Somehow stop it so I do not have to sign."

Just before we got to the closing, my realtor called, "Dr. Murdock, I hate to tell you this, but the seller has made one more request. If you do not do this, he will not sell you the property."

I said, "Really?" The Holy Spirit intervened.

Never Stay Where There Is An Absence of Favor.

Create Your Secret Place

Sanctify a place in your home where you meet at the same time every day with The Holy Spirit.

Habit Is More Powerful Than Desire.

Habit is the ability to do something twice. God uses habit. Jesus went to the temple as was His custom. (See Luke 4:16.) David prayed 7 times a day. (See Psalm 119:164.) Daniel prayed 3 times a day. (See Daniel 6:10.)

Your presence is a photograph of your passion for Him.

You do not have to change the tone of your voice.

You do not have to act spiritual. You do not even have to yell. Just enter His Presence.

The most important thing in prayer is showing up.

Do not worry about how to pray. Do not worry about approaching God the "right" way. *Just show up.*

Use your energy to *enter* His Presence. Let Him use His energy to *keep* you there.

Always enter singing. A song is the protocol for entering the spirit world. *A Song Is A Corridor Into The Presence of God.*

Four Months Later...

Four months later I was involved in another real estate transaction. I got up on a Saturday morning and went to my Secret Place.

As I was praying in the Spirit, I said, "Lord, give me a plan. Give me *Your* plan." And He gave me His plan. I called the attorneys. Two hours later, I had a magnificent financial profit.

That is not bad for two hours.

Actually, I do not think it is bad for a whole year.

The Holy Spirit will give you plans. That is the importance of sitting in His Presence.

One Hour In The Presence of God Will Reveal The Flaws of Your Most Carefully Laid Plans.

It takes a *moment* to get a *Command.*

It takes *hours* sometimes to get *The Plan.*

Always remember that a Divine Plan is *as important as* the Anointing. You can be an anointed man of God and *miss* The Plan. Joshua was anointed, yet he lost the battle of Ai. He was anointed, but he did not obey The Plan. (See Joshua 8.)

It is not enough just to build an ark. You have got to build *the ark according to The Plan.*

It is not enough to build the temple. You have got to build *the temple according to The Plan.*

It is not enough to build the tabernacle. You have got to build *the tabernacle according to The Plan.*

The purpose of God's Presence is for His Plan to become obvious. You may receive a command and then leave His Presence, but you must get The Plan.

The Bible is a book about plans.

The Holy Spirit will talk to you about a plan in His

Presence. He will expose the hidden agenda of untrustworthy people in your life.

Always remember this. Everybody fails because of *one* thing...trusting the *wrong* voice. If you succeed, it will be because you trusted the *right* voice.

Your Future Is Decided By Who You Choose To Believe.

Master Keys For Your Secret Place Experience

▶ *God Rules The Universe Through Conversation.*
▶ *The Path of Favor Is The Will of God.*
▶ *Never Stay Where There Is An Absence of Favor.*
▶ *Habit Is More Powerful Than Desire.*
▶ *A Song Is A Corridor Into The Presence of God.*
▶ *One Hour In The Presence of God Will Reveal The Flaws of Your Most Carefully Laid Plans.*
▶ *Your Future Is Decided By Who You Choose To Believe.*

RECOMMENDED INVESTMENTS:
The Holy Spirit Handbook (Book/B-100/153 pg/$15)
Where Miracles Are Born (Book/B-115/32 pg/$7)
The Greatest Day of My Life (Book/B-116/32 pg/$7)

7

YOUR DECISION TO SOW SEED WITH EXPECTATION OF A SPECIFIC HARVEST

Everybody Sows.

You cannot stop yourself from sowing. Every day of your life you *will* sow. You will either sow *nothing* or you will sow *something*.

There will never be a day in your life that you do not sow. *Never.* Time. Energy.

A Seed of Nothing Produces A Season of Nothing.

In The Old Testament, even the poorest of the poor had to sow something; a turtledove, a pigeon or a meal. "...none shall appear before Me empty," (Exodus 23:15).

▶ *Words Are The Seeds...For Feelings.*

▶ *Battle Is The Seed...For Territory.*

▶ *Honor Is The Seed...For Access.*

▶ *Listening Is The Seed...For Knowledge.*

▶ *Knowledge Is The Seed...For Change.*

Changes In Your Life Are Always Proportionate To Knowledge.

The purpose of knowledge is to create a change.

Many people understand The Tithe...the 10 percent of our income...the *holy* part that *purifies* the remaining 90 percent of our money.

I heard an interesting statistic some months ago. Within 6 weeks any new money printed in America has been touched by every known disease. People have become ill handling money. This is why I believe that my Tithe and my Offerings are the *spiritual circumcision* of my financial life...the cutting away of what does not belong to me.

When I return 10 percent to God, He *purifies* the remaining 90 percent...*authorizing* it to be *fertile* and *reproductive* in His world.

I have not met a Christian who does not give.

I have met very few who know to sow with *expectation* for a *specific* Harvest. The Harvest comes from expectation.

The Seed alone is not enough.

It is possible to sow without expectation. It is possible to sow into a ministry because the ministry needs your help, but *you must sow with expectation of a Harvest.*

Expectation...The Secret of The Harvest

The secret of the Harvest is not the Seed.

The secret of the Harvest is my *Expectations*... wrapped around my Seed. "He that cometh to God must believe that He is, and that He is a Rewarder of them that diligently seek Him," (Hebrews 11:6).

The *Seed* is what God multiplies.

My *Expectation* is why.

Remember Elijah's conversation with the widow in 1 Kings 17? He began to paint a picture of the Harvest in her Mind. He gave the widow a *reason* to sow...*a motive.* "For thus saith the Lord God of Israel, The barrel of meal shall not waste, neither shall the cruse of oil fail, until the day that the Lord sendeth rain upon the earth," (1 Kings 17:14).

Are You Expecting Your Harvest..?

A man walked up to me. "Brother Mike, when I give to God, I expect nothing in return."

I said, "I wrote a song for you. 'How dumb thou art. How dumb thou art!'"

Faith Is Expectation Wrapped Around My Seed.

In Mark 10, Peter mutters something, and Jesus turns around and says, "What did you say?"

"We have given up everything to follow You."

Jesus could have said, "I know. Three catfish and a boat." But He did not. Jesus looked at Peter and said, "Anything you give up will come back to you one hundredfold." (See Mark 10:28-30.)

Conversation Reveals Expectations

If I hear you talk, I know what you are expecting.

Expectation is a magnet. In Malachi 3, God gives an instruction: "Bring Me The Tithe And Offerings."

In the next verse He explains why. Did He say, "Because the angels are eating more than we ever dreamed?" No.

God promises to stop the theft in your life. "Bring ye all the tithes into the storehouse, that there may be meat in Mine house, and prove Me now herewith, saith the Lord of hosts, if I will not open you the windows of Heaven, and pour you out a blessing, that there shall not be room enough to receive it. And I will rebuke the devourer for your sakes, and he shall not destroy the fruits of your ground; neither shall your vine cast her fruit before the time in the field, saith the Lord of hosts," (Malachi 3:10-11).

Expectation Is The Only Magnet That Attracts The Miracle Provision God Has Promised.

$65,000 In 14 Days...

A lady in Knoxville, Tennessee, came to a service I was conducting. I did not know her. I had instructed the congregation, "When you present your Seed to the Lord tonight, write on your check what you want your Harvest to be. Your Seed is a conversation with God."

She came to me after the service and said, "I hope this thing works because my ex-husband has not paid me a penny of child support in 15 years."

I said, "Did you write his name on the check?"

"Yes, I did." Fourteen days later, he sent her a check for $65,000. *She sowed with expectation.*

A $26,622 Medical Bill Paid In Full...

I sent my mother and father a tape where I shared about a Seed God was dealing with my ministry about. I said, "Mama and Daddy, if you never sow again, sow this Seed."

My mother called, "Baby, I felt God speaking to me on that tape."

I said, "Mama, there is something to this."

She said, "Son, we need a Miracle." I knew they did. She had a double by-pass surgery in a hospital in Houston, Texas. The medical bill was $48,000. They had emptied their savings and got it down to $26,622.

She called me a week later, "Baby, I sent my check, but I have not seen any Miracles."

I replied, "My lord, Mama, give God a chance. It has just been one week."

Seed...Time...Harvest..!

Harvest never follows sowing.
Waiting follows sowing.
Waiting Is The Proof of Trust.
Mama called me during the second week. "Son, it has been two weeks. I still have not seen any Miracles. Was I supposed to write the Miracle on the left-hand side of the check or on the right-hand side of the check? I think I may have written it on the wrong side of the check."

At the end of the third week, there were 3 messages on my answering machine. I was to call home.

When I called them back, my father got on one line and my mother on the other. He said, "Son, I can hardly catch my breath. We have just been on the phone with the hospital. We received a letter from them. They wrote, 'Your bill of $26,622 just came to our attention. Once in a while we want to do something good for somebody. We have decided to mark your bill paid-in-full!'"

That Texas Hospital gave my mother and father $26,622.

It Happened In Daytona Beach, Florida...

During a service in Daytona Beach, Florida, I instructed the people, "Write on your check where you want to see your Harvest."

A young man on the platform wrote, "A gorgeous

wife." A young lady that had never met him was on the back row and she wrote down, "A godly husband."

They met 3 days later.

They had 3 children! As I sat at their table for a meal, she laughingly said, "Tell people to be very careful what they write on those checks!"

It Happened In Knoxville, Tennessee...

A woman walked up to me with her tall, lanky husband. She said, "Remember that Seed you told us to plant and write our name on it."

I said, "Yes ma'am."

She said, "This is him."

For 20 years, he had never been to church with her. He gave his life to Jesus two weeks after she wrote his name on a Seed. *The Power of The Seed.*

Your Seed Is The Only Influence You Have Over Your Future.

A Debt-Free House In 8 Months...

On a Wednesday night in Chicago, a preacher stood up and said, "How many would like to be debt-free?"

Debt can choke and suffocate you. *Debt Is Emptying Your Future To Fill Your Present.* The Lord can give you a debt-free home and a debt-free lifestyle. Never again will you be under the *burden* of credit and debt.

Then the preacher said, "How many would like a debt-free house?"

I have had news reporters in helicopters flying over my house taking pictures. They have posted pictures of my house on the internet and in newspapers. I did not know how pretty my house was until I saw it in the newspaper. I thought, "God has been good to me." I had forgotten how good God has been to me.

He said, "Plant a Seed equal to one month's mortgage payment. Write on the check *debt-free home in 12 months*. Hold it in your left hand and slap it 3 times." Because he was a man of God, I wrote on the check as he had instructed, then held it in my hand and slapped it 3 times...in total obedience to an unusual instruction.

In 8 months my house was miraculously debt-free.
▶ *The Purpose of The Seed Is To Birth A Harvest.*
▶ *When I Let Go of What Is In My Hand, God Will Let Go of What Is In His Hand.*
▶ *The Seed That Leaves Your Hand Never Leaves Your Life; It Enters Your Future Where It Multiplies.*
▶ *When I Let Go of Something I Can See, God Releases Something I Cannot See.*
▶ *If I Keep What I Have, That Is My Harvest. If I Sow It, It Is My Seed. I Can Create Any Future I Want With My Seed.*
▶ *Your Future Will Have To Obey Your Seed.*
▶ *Your Seed Is The Only Authority Your Future Obeys.*

3 Harvests You Should Expect From Your Seed...

1. Debt-Free Home. I want God to give you a debt-free house that makes you like a trophy on display to your entire family. (This is what my Jehovah-Jireh has done in my life.)

A Debt-Free House That No Government Can Take Away From You.

I want God to give you a house that agitates your enemies...*a house that your enemies take pictures of.*

If your enemy has not thought about you this month, you are not blessed yet. Your enemy needs to think about you sometime.

The Focus of God Becomes The Focus of Satan.

You Too Can Have A Debt-Free Lifestyle...

God can give you a debt-free lifestyle.

From this day forward, make a decision to use cash for everything that you buy.

A few weeks ago, my banker asked me, "Why don't you ever borrow any money from us?"

I said, "I hate debt. I like paying cash."

The Wisdom Center is debt-free.

We have a Jehovah-Jireh in our life.

2. A 7-Fold Return On Anything Satan Has Stolen From You.

There has been *continuous* theft in your life.

There has never been a day in your life that satan has not *attempted* to steal something from you that God wanted to happen in your life. There is a lot that God has sent that never arrived at your house.

Anything Good Is Hated By Everything Evil.

There are 8 levels of sowing where I have seen *radical* results. The Seed that has created the *quickest* result for me has been the Seed of $1,000. I have sown larger Seed, but the Harvest took longer.

The $1,000 Seed level is where I began to see *radical* and *immediate* Favor unlike anything I had ever experienced. The *dominant reward* of the $1,000 Seed has been *Favor.*

You do not need everybody liking you...*just the right person.* You are *one* person away from the season you are craving and desiring.

The Difference In Seasons Is A *Person.*

When I know who likes you, I can predict your Future.

Joseph did not need everybody liking him...*just one person. Only Pharaoh.* (See Genesis 41:37-45.)

God Gives Seed To The Sower...

God promised to give Seed to the sower.

God may give it to you $100 at a time...or even $200 at a time. "Now He that ministereth seed to the sower both minister bread for your food, and multiply your seed sown, and increase the fruits of your righteousness," (2 Corinthians 9:10).

When God Talks To You About A Seed, He Has A Harvest On His Mind.

3.   The Boaz Anointing.

The Anointing You Respect Is The Anointing That Increases In Your Life.

The Anointing You Respect Is The Anointing You Attract.

Ruth so respected the anointing that was on Boaz, she received everything he had. "And she said, I pray you, let me glean and gather after the reapers among the sheaves: so she came, and hath continued even from the morning until now, that she tarried a little in the house. Then said Boaz unto Ruth, Hearest thou not, my daughter? Go not to glean in another field, neither go from hence, but abide here fast by my maidens," (Ruth 2:7-8). "So Boaz took Ruth, and she was his wife: and when he went in unto her, the Lord gave her conception, and she bare a son. And the women said unto Naomi, Blessed be the Lord, Which hath not left thee this day without a kinsman, that his name may be famous in Israel," (Ruth 3:13-14).

As you sow your Seed of $1,000, believe God for the Boaz anointing over your life. Every time God gives me a Miracle, *may He give you a Miracle*. Every time God blesses me, *may He bless you*.

Today Is The Poorest You Will Ever Be The Rest of Your Life..!

Do not negotiate with The Holy Spirit.

Only a fool will argue with a Giver. The $1,000 Seed may be money you have set aside for a new car or equity in a home.

Incidentally, I love to remind our Partners that every Seed of $1,000 is a Million-Soul Seed...because it provides TV airtime coverage to one million homes.

Wrap expectation around your Seed...for a *specific* Harvest.

My Special Prayer For Your Harvest...

"Holy Spirit, if what I have said about sowing and reaping is just for Mike Murdock's personal gain, may a curse be on me and my ministry and may my tongue cleave to the roof of my mouth. If what I have said about The Law of The Seed and The Harvest is Your Word, I agree that within 12 months, there will be double Wisdom...double Favor...double Finances.

"I set myself in agreement with my special friend, as he presents this Seed of $1,000 to reach a million souls. I set myself in agreement for a debt-free home and a debt-free lifestyle.

"I decree a sevenfold return over everything satan has stolen. I set myself in agreement for a Boaz anointing. Every time You give me a car, give them a car. When you give me a jet, give them a jet. Do the supernatural. I set myself in covenant in The Name of Jesus.

"Lord, I know that if we keep what we have, that is our Harvest. If we sow it, it is our Seed. We do not want another year like last year. We want this year to be different. We launch this year with new Seed.

"Father, I ask You within 8 days let the first wave of Harvest come. Eight is the number of new beginnings. Let the first Harvest begin to come within 8 days from the time they sow this Seed. Do it so supernaturally they never forget it. In Jesus' Name."

Everything I Have Came From God...

I do not have anything God did not give me.

Say these words aloud, "Holy Spirit, thank You for everything You have given to me. Thank You for my eyesight, my hearing, my health, my family, my job, my ministry. Thank You for Your blessings.

"Today I enter into Partnership with You. I am a receiver of an Uncommon Anointing. This year my Wisdom will double...my Favor will double...my Finances will double. In the Name of Jesus, I speak to this Seed, 'Seed, listen to me. Go into my Future. Multiply and come back to me with a hundredfold return.'"

Picture the hundredfold return. Begin to thank your Jehovah-Jireh. Even more important than the $1,000 Seed is for you to picture the Harvest you want to see.

May I share what is happening for those who boldly expect their Divine Harvest as they plant their Seeds into God's Work..?

It Happened In New York...

A few weeks ago, I met with about 300 of my strongest partners in New York. A woman and her husband stood to speak, "We are pastors here in New York. We heard you talk on television about the $1,000 Seed. You had broken the back of poverty with a $1,000 Seed. We did not even have $1,000, but I shared with my husband that we needed to sow it."

They borrowed $1,000 to sow. Thirty days later their church received a gift of $100 million. *$100 million in 30 days!*

The Miracle of The Lifetime Blessing...

I was preaching for Rod Parsley in Columbus, Ohio. Just before that I had given away everything I had. There have been 3 times in my life God told me to sow everything I owned.

I had just received an $8,500 royalty check.

I was excited. That night The Holy Spirit spoke to me to plant that Seed of $8,500.

It was everything I had.

Six weeks later, on a Tuesday morning, at 7:15, at the Hyatt Regency Hotel in Houston, Texas, God gave me an idea. I called a friend and he said, "If you will let me run with it, I will pay you royalties every 90 days."

He put the product in Wal-Mart, K-Mart and Hallmark. Every 90 days I started getting a royalty check. God gave me a *lifetime* income.

The first royalty check built me a gymnasium at my house. The next royalty check bought me a beautiful black-on-black Rolls Royce. *I paid cash.*

Are You One of The 300 Uncommon Millionaires..?

I have asked the Lord to raise up 300 millionaires under our teaching. We have 20 so far.

You know you are poor if you think a million dollars is a lot! If God starts to bless you, a million is just the *starting* place!

If God wants to do something great through your life, a million will not be enough.

I have lost money in oil.

I have lost money in real estate.

I have never lost money investing in God.

How close are you to the supernatural? Closer than you have ever dreamed. I would like for God to take the same anointing that is on my life and place it on someone else to become *trophies on display* of what God can do.

Your dreams are a lot bigger than $8,500.

The Seed of $8,500 is not for everybody, but there are those who would like for God to give them a lifetime income like He gave me.

A lifetime blessing…that they would never have to

worry about their family again for the rest of their life. *When You Ask God For A Miracle, He Will Always Give You An Instruction.*

My Prayer For Your Lifetime Blessing...

"Father, as they plant the Seed of $8,500 in recognition of Your Greatness and Your Goodness, I pray that they will receive the same grace and anointing that You have placed on my life.

"The Sunday night I planted that $8,500 Seed, it was everything that I had to my name. But You spoke to my heart to explore and experiment with what You could do with my $8,500. And the blessing has been profound. What we can walk away from we have mastered. What we cannot walk away from has mastered us.

"As they sow their Seed, I release the $8,500 Seed for the sake of The Gospel. As they sow into this anointing and world missions, may the same grace come upon them. In Jesus' Name, Amen."

76 Wisdom Keys of Mike Murdock In This Book

1. A Song Is A Corridor Into The Presence of God.
2. An Uncommon Future Requires An Uncommon Mentor.
3. Anything Good Is Hated By Everything Evil.
4. Battle Is The Seed...For Territory.
5. Celebration Is The Proof of Honor.
6. Changes In Your Life Are Always Proportionate To Knowledge.
7. Conversation Is The Birthplace For Seasons.
8. Debt Is Emptying Your Future To Fill Your Present.
9. Divine Provision Is Only Guaranteed At The Place of Your Assignment.
10. Doubt Authorizes Satanic Attack In Your Life.
11. Doubt Produces Pain Like Faith Produces Miracles.
12. Doubt Produces Tragedies As Quickly As Faith Produces Miracles.
13. Every Miracle Begins With A Conversation.
14. Every Sin On Earth Is A Sin of Dishonor.
15. Every Tragedy Begins With A Conversation.
16. Everybody Sees Something You Do Not See.
17. Everything Created Solves A Problem.
18. Everything Good Is Hated By Everything Evil.
19. Expectation Is The Only Magnet That Attracts The Miracle Provision God Has Promised.
20. Faith Is Expectation Wrapped Around My Seed.
21. Faith Is The Only Voice God Respects.
22. Go Where You Are Celebrated Instead of Where You Are Tolerated.

23. God Made Places Before He Made People.
24. God Rules The Universe Through Conversation.
25. God's Only Pain Is To Be Doubted; God's Only Pleasure Is To Be Believed.
26. Habit Is More Powerful Than Desire.
27. Honor Is The Seed...For Access.
28. Honor Must Become Your Seed Before You Reap It As A Harvest.
29. Honoring Parents Guarantees Generational Blessing.
30. Knowledge Is The Seed...For Change.
31. Listening Is The Seed...For Knowledge.
32. Mentorship Is The Transference of Knowledge.
33. Mentorship Is Wisdom Without The Pain.
34. Money Is Merely A Reward For Solving A Problem.
35. Money Is Waiting For You...At Your Place of Assignment.
36. Never Stay Where There Is An Absence of Favor.
37. One Hour In The Presence of God Will Reveal The Flaws of Your Most Carefully Laid Plans.
38. Questions Are The Seeds For Wisdom.
39. Questions Host Answers On The Earth; Answers Only Respond To Questions.
40. Questions Schedule Events On The Earth.
41. The Anointing You Respect Is The Anointing That Increases In Your Life.
42. The Anointing You Respect Is The Anointing You Attract.
43. The Divine Purpose For Authority Is Order.
44. The Focus of God Becomes The Focus of Satan.
45. The Future of Every Man Is Determined By The Woman He Trusts.
46. The Path of Favor Is The Will of God.

47. The Proof of Love Is The Investment of Time.
48. The Proofs of Legitimate Authority Are Provision, Protection And Promotion.
49. The Purpose of The Seed Is To Birth A Harvest.
50. The Role of Wisdom Is Correct Reactions.
51. The Seed That Leaves Your Hand Never Leaves Your Life; It Enters Your Future Where It Multiplies.
52. The Size of Your Enemy Reveals The Size of Your Rewards.
53. The Word of God Is The Wisdom of God.
54. Waiting Is The Proof of Trust.
55. Warfare Is The Proof An Enemy Has Discerned Your Future.
56. What Enters You Determines What Exits You.
57. When God Talks To You About A Seed, He Has A Harvest On His Mind.
58. When I Let Go of Something I Can See, God Releases Something I Cannot See.
59. When I Let Go of What Is In My Hand, God Will Let Go of What Is In His Hand.
60. When You Ask God For A Miracle, He Will Always Give You An Instruction.
61. When You Solve A Problem, You Schedule A Reward.
62. When You Want Something You Have Never Had, You Must Do Something You Have Never Done.
63. Wisdom Is The Ability To Recognize Difference. Honor Is The Willingness To Reward Someone For Their Difference.
64. Words Are The Seeds...For Feelings.
65. You Can Only Be Promoted By The Person You Serve.

66. You Never Outgrow Warfare; You Must Simply Learn To Fight.
67. You Will Only Have Significant Success In Something That Is An Obsession.
68. Your Assignment Is Always The Problem God Has Designed You To Solve For Others.
69. Your Assignment Is Not Your Decision – But Your Discovery.
70. Your Decisions Decide Your Success.
71. Your Faith Decides Your Experiences.
72. Your Future Is Decided By Who You Choose To Believe.
73. Your Greatness Is Not Hidden To The One God Has Assigned To Promote You.
74. Your Reaction To Your Parents Determines God's Reaction To You.
75. Your Seed Is The Only Influence You Have Over Your Future.
76. Your Victories Are Hidden In The Mistakes of Your Enemy.

DECISION

Will You Accept Jesus As Your Personal Savior Today?

The Bible says, "That if thou shalt confess with thy mouth the Lord Jesus, and shalt believe in thine heart that God hath raised Him from the dead, thou shalt be saved," (Romans 10:9).

Pray this prayer from your heart today!

"Dear Jesus, I believe that You died for me and rose again on the third day. I confess I am a sinner...I need Your love and forgiveness...Come into my heart. Forgive my sins. I receive Your eternal life. Confirm Your love by giving me peace, joy and supernatural love for others. Amen."

DR. MIKE MURDOCK

is in tremendous demand as one of the most dynamic speakers in America today.

More than 17,000 audiences in over 100 countries have attended his Schools of Wisdom and conferences. Hundreds of invitations come to him from churches, colleges and business corporations. He is a noted author of over 250 books, including the best sellers, *The Leadership Secrets of Jesus* and *Secrets of the Richest Man Who Ever Lived.* Thousands view his weekly television program, *Wisdom Keys with Mike Murdock.* Many attend his Schools of Wisdom that he hosts in many cities of America.

☐ Yes, Mike! I made a decision to accept Christ as my personal Savior today. Please send me my free gift of your book, *31 Keys to a New Beginning* to help me with my new life in Christ.

NAME _____ BIRTHDAY _____

ADDRESS _____

CITY _____ STATE ___ ZIP _____

PHONE _____ E-MAIL _____

Mail to: **The Wisdom Center** · 4051 Denton Hwy. · Ft. Worth, TX 76117
1-817-759-BOOK · 1-817-759-2665 · 1-817-759-0300
You Will Love Our Website..! WisdomOnline.com

DR. MIKE MURDOCK

1 Has embraced his Assignment to Pursue...Proclaim...and Publish the Wisdom of God to help people achieve their dreams and goals.

2 Preached his first public sermon at the age of 8.

3 Preached his first evangelistic crusade at the age of 15.

4 Began full-time evangelism at the age of 19, which has continued since 1966.

5 Has traveled and spoken to more than 17,000 audiences in over 100 countries, including East and West Africa, Asia, Europe and South America.

6 Noted author of over 250 books, including best sellers, *Wisdom for Winning, Dream Seeds, The Double Diamond Principle, The Law of Recognition* and *The Holy Spirit Handbook.*

7 Created the popular *Topical Bible* series for Businessmen, Mothers, Fathers, Teenagers; *The One-Minute Pocket Bible* series, and *The Uncommon Life* series.

8 The Creator of The Master 7 Mentorship System, an Achievement Program for Believers.

9 Has composed thousands of songs such as "I Am Blessed," "You Can Make It," "God Rides On Wings Of Love" and "Jesus, Just The Mention Of Your Name," recorded by many gospel artists.

10 Is the Founder and Senior Pastor of The Wisdom Center, in Fort Worth, Texas...a Church with International Ministry around the world.

11 Host of *Wisdom Keys with Mike Murdock,* a weekly TV Program seen internationally.

12 Has appeared often on TBN, CBN, BET, Daystar, Inspirational Network, LeSea Broadcasting and other television network programs.

13 Has led over 3,000 to accept the call into full-time ministry.

48

THE MINISTRY

1 **Wisdom Books & Literature** - Over 250 best-selling Wisdom Books and 70 Teaching Tape Series.

2 **Church Crusades** - Multitudes are ministered to in crusades and seminars throughout America in "The Uncommon Wisdom Conferences." Known as a man who loves pastors he has focused on church crusades for over 43 years.

3 **Music Ministry** - Millions have been blessed by the anointed songwriting and singing of Mike Murdock, who has made over 15 music albums and CDs available.

4 **Television** - *Wisdom Keys with Mike Murdock,* a nationally-syndicated weekly television program.

5 **The Wisdom Center** - The Church and Ministry Offices where Dr. Murdock speaks weekly on Wisdom for The Uncommon Life.

6 **Schools of The Holy Spirit** - Mike Murdock hosts Schools of The Holy Spirit in many churches to mentor believers on the Person and Companionship of The Holy Spirit.

7 **Schools of Wisdom** - In many major cities Mike Murdock hosts Schools of Wisdom for those who want personalized and advanced training for achieving "The Uncommon Dream."

8 **Missions Outreach** - Dr. Mike Murdock's overseas outreaches to over 100 countries have included crusades in East and West Africa, Asia, Europe and South America.

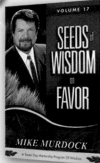

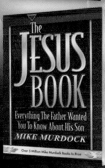

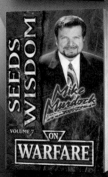

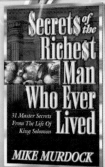

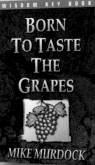

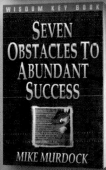

Career 7

Book Pak For Business People!

DR. MIKE MURDOCK

① The Businessman's Topical Bible (Book/B-33/384pg/$10)

② 31 Secrets for Career Success (Book/B-44/114pg/$10)

③ 31 Scriptures Every Businessman Should Memorize (Book/B-141/32pg/$3)

④ 7 Overlooked Keys To Effective Goal-Setting (Book/B-127/32pg/$7)

⑤ 7 Rewards of Problem Solving (Book/B-118/32pg/$7)

⑥ How To Double Your Productivity In 24 Hours (Book/B-137/32pg/$7)

⑦ The Mentor's Manna on Achievement (Book/B-79/32pg/$5)

Each Wisdom Book may be purchased separately if so desired.

D **THE WISDOM CENTER** 4051 Denton Highway • Fort Worth, TX 76117

1-817-759-BOOK
1-817-759-2665
1-817-759-0300

You Will Love Our Website..!
WISDOMONLINE.COM

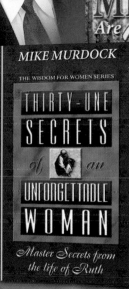

Millionaire-Talk

Increase 4
Book Pak!

❶ The Book That Changed My Life... (Book/B-117/32pg/$7)

❷ Secrets of The Journey, Vol. 2 (Book/B-93/32pg/$5)

❸ 7 Keys to 1000 Times More
(Book/B-104/128pg/$10)

❹ 31 Secrets for Career Success
(Book/B-44/114pg/$10)

Each Wisdom Book may be purchased separately if so desired.

The Wisdom Center
Increase 4 Book Pak!
Only $**20** $32 Value
PAK-26
Wisdom Is The Principal Thing

Add 20% For S/H

THE WISDOM CENTER
4051 Denton Highway · Fort Worth, TX 76117

1-817-759-**BOOK**
1-817-759-2665
1-817-759-0300

You Will Love Our Website..!
WISDOMONLINE.COM

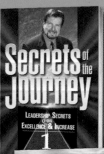

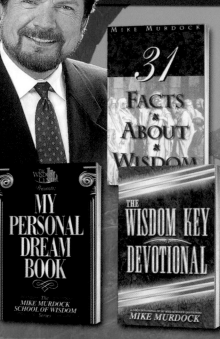

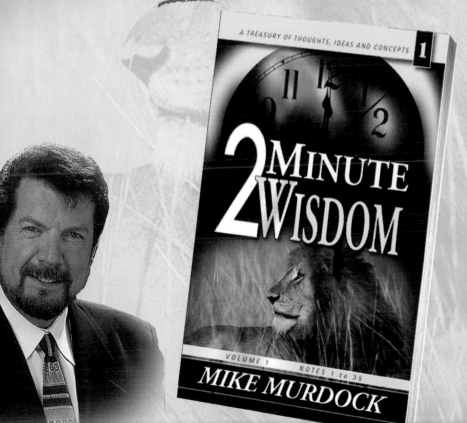

THE WISDOM BIBLE

Partnership Edition

Over 120 Wisdom Study Guides Included Such As:

- ▸ *10 Qualities of Uncommon Achievers*
- ▸ *18 Facts You Should Know About The Anointing*
- ▸ *21 Facts To Help You Identify Those Assigned To You*
- ▸ *31 Facts You Should Know About Your Assignment*
- ▸ *8 Keys That Unlock Victory In Every Attack*
- ▸ *22 Defense Techniques To Remember During Seasons of Personal Attack*
- ▸ *20 Wisdom Keys And Techniques To Remember During An Uncommon Battle*
- ▸ *11 Benefits You Can Expect From God*
- ▸ *31 Facts You Should Know About Favor*
- ▸ *The Covenant of 58 Blessings*
- ▸ *7 Keys To Receiving Your Miracle*
- ▸ *16 Facts You Should Remember About Contentious People*
- ▸ *5 Facts Solomon Taught About Contracts*
- ▸ *7 Facts You Should Know About Conflict*
- ▸ *6 Steps That Can Unlock Your Self-Confidence*
- ▸ *And Much More!*

Your Partnership makes such a difference in The Wisdom Center Outreach Ministries. I wanted to place a Gift in your hand that could last a lifetime for you and your family...**The Wisdom Study Bible.**

40 Years of Personal Notes...this Partnership Edition Bible contains 160 pages of my Personal Study Notes...that could forever change your Bible Study of The Word of God. This **Partnership Edition**...is my personal **Gift of Appreciation** when you sow your Sponsorship Seed of $1,000 to help us complete The Prayer Center and TV Studio Complex. An Uncommon Seed Always Creates An Uncommon Harvest!

Mike

Thank you from my heart for your Seed of Obedience (Luke 6:38).